YOUNG ARCHITECT

Storybook Homes

by Gerry Bailey

Illustrated by Joelle Dreidemy and Karen Radford

Crabtree Publishing Company

Crabtree Publishing Company
www.crabtreebooks.com
1-800-387-7650

Published in Canada
616 Welland Ave.
St. Catharines, ON
L2M 5V6

Published in the United States
PMB 59051, 350 Fifth Ave.
59th Floor,
New York, NY

Author: Gerry Bailey
Illustrators: Joelle Dreidemy and Karen Radford
Project coordinator: Kelly McNiven
Editor: Kathy Middleton
Proofreader: Crystal Sikkens
**Print and Production coordinator and
    Prepress technician:** Margaret Amy Salter

Photographs:
Pg 4   Asier Villafranca
Pg 10   (tl) S.john; (tr) jennyt; (b) Alehnia
Pg 11   (t)Bork; (m) mambo6435; (b) Neirfy
Pg 18   (t) David Hughes; (bl) Goran Bogicevic /
            Shutterstock.com; (br)Tomasz Szymanski
Pg 20   Haines Shoe House, Penn.
Pg 22   Malgorzata Kistrn
Pg 24/25   © eddie linssen / Alamy
Pg 28   (l) meunierd; (r) FotograFFF
Pg 29   Rafal Olechowski

All images are Shutterstock.com unless otherwise stated.

Every attempt has been made to clear copyright. Should
there be any inadvertent omission, please apply to the
publisher for rectification.

Printed in Hong Kong/092013/BK20130703

Library and Archives Canada Cataloguing in Publication

Bailey, Gerry, author
        Storybook homes / by Gerry Bailey ; illustrated by Joelle Dreidemy
and Karen Radford.

(Young architect)
Includes index.
Issued in print and electronic formats.
ISBN 978-0-7787-0288-7 (bound).--ISBN 978-0-7787-0298-6 (pbk.).--
ISBN 978-1-4271-1277-4 (pdf).--ISBN 978-1-4271-1273-6 (html)

        1. Fantastic architecture--Juvenile literature. 2. Architecture, Domestic--
Juvenile literature. I. Dreidemy, Joelle, illustrator II. Radford, Karen,
illustrator III. Title.

NA209.5.B33 2013   j728   C2013-904073-0
                                                            C2013-904074-9

Library of Congress Cataloging-in-Publication Data

Bailey, Gerry.
 Storybook homes / Written by Gerry Bailey ; Illustrated by Joelle Dreidemy
and Karen Radford.
        pages cm. -- (Young architect)
 Includes index.
 ISBN 978-0-7787-0288-7 (reinforced library binding) -- ISBN 978-0-7787-0298-6 (pbk.) --
ISBN 978-1-4271-1277-4 (electronic pdf) -- ISBN 978-1-4271-1273-6 (electronic html)
1. Fantastic architecture--Juvenile literature. 2. Architecture, Domestic--Juvenile
literature. I. Dreidemy, Joelle, illustrator. II. Title.

 NA209.5.B35 2013
 728--dc23

                        2013023900

Contents

Introduction

Where do you live—in an apartment building, a townhouse, a house in the country? Does it sound a bit ordinary? What if you lived somewhere really special like in a fairytale castle with tall **spires** and **steeples**, for example?

Or perhaps you would prefer to live in a tall tower?
How about a roomy old shoe?
Well, your wish has just come true! Now you can be a young architect and design a house right out of your favorite storybook.

King Ludwig's castle

More than 150 years ago, King Ludwig II of Bavaria decided to build himself a spectacular castle high up on a rock overlooking a beautiful lake in Germany.

The king planned the castle of his dreams based on German fairy tales he had read as a boy. It would be built of sparkling white stone and have tall, gleaming towers with delicate cone-shaped roofs, or spires.

Surrounded by dark forests and snowy mountains, he wanted it to seem like a fairytale castle towering over the valley below.

Ludwig started by making a list of the features he wanted in his castle.

King Ludwig's castle is called Schloss Neuschwanstein. It is in Bavaria, Germany.

The rooms

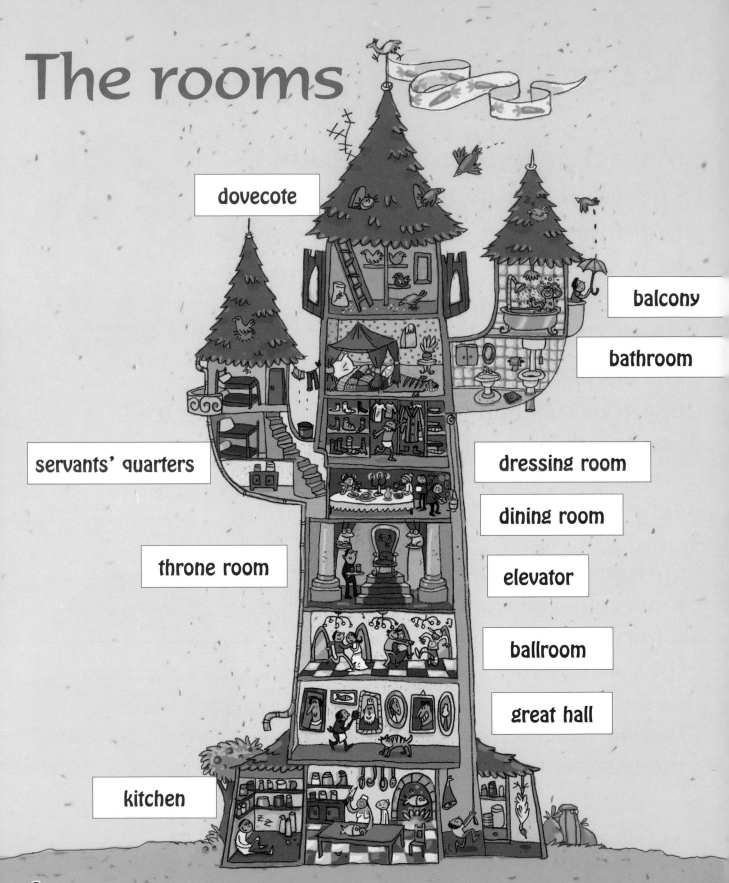

dovecote

balcony

bathroom

servants' quarters

dressing room

dining room

throne room

elevator

ballroom

great hall

kitchen

6

I want to keep birds in a dovecote under the roof.

I want my own private balcony.

I want my bedroom to have a four-poster bed
and a bathroom next door.

My dressing room should be large enough
to keep 100 jackets, 52 pairs of pants
and 44 pairs of boots.

The servants' **quarters** should be close by.

The ballroom must have glass **chandeliers**
and a marble floor for dancing.

I need a large throne room to greet my guests.

One hundred family portraits will hang in the great hall.

The kitchen will have a huge fireplace,
a roasting **spit**, and a bread oven.

An elevator will carry hot meals from the
kitchen to the dining room.

Architect's notebook

- The structure -

spire and steeple

roof

King Ludwig wants a design that looks like a medieval castle—the kind you would find in old-fashioned fairy tales with brave knights who fought fierce dragons.

window

arch

The shape and style of a building is known as its **structure**.

The individual parts of the building are known as structural features.

pillars

parapet

turret

balcony

Which of these structural features can you find on the castle drawing on the next page?

stone sculpture

8

The building materials

Buildings are made using many different materials.

COLORED **GLASS** is used to decorate windows. Glass is made by heating a special sand until it becomes a liquid, then cooling it.

SLATE is a smooth, flat stone often used as roof **tiles**.

LIMESTONE is a white stone that is easily carved into shapes. Limestone is **porous**, which means it absorbs water.

MARBLE is a beautiful, sparkling stone with a surface that is very shiny when it is polished.

TIMBER is obtained by cutting down trees and sawing the logs into planks, or flat boards, at a sawmill.

CONCRETE is made from a mixture of cement and crushed rocks. It dries into a very hard material used to make the foundations and walls of buildings.

On site

King Ludwig wants his castle to be built high up on the edge of a deep gorge. This will make it difficult to bring heavy building materials up the steep sides of the valley to the **site**.

Architect's notebook

The site plan

This site **plan** shows where the castle will be built—perched on the edge of a steep gorge. It shows the land around it, including the forests and the lake.

slabs of slate

marble

wooden planks

Colored glass must be carried carefully.

Cement is made by mixing sand and limestone.

13

The floor plans

The architect has drawn up a floor plan. This shows which rooms will be located on the ground floor of the castle and which on the floors above and below.

- Architect's words -

SCALE:
The architect's drawing must be done to **scale**. This means that every unit of measurement on the drawing will stand for a larger unit of measurement on the ground.

Ground-Floor Plan

1. Main entrance
2. Courtyard and
   stables
3. **Archway**
4. Courtyard and
   winter garden
5. Great hall and
   portrait gallery

First-Floor Plan

1. Balcony
2. Ballroom
3. Throne room
4. Staircase to
   second floor

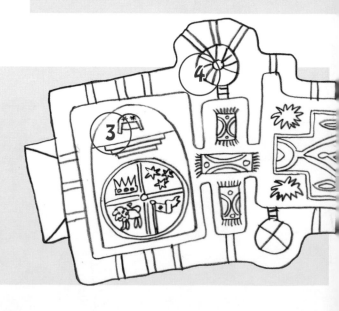

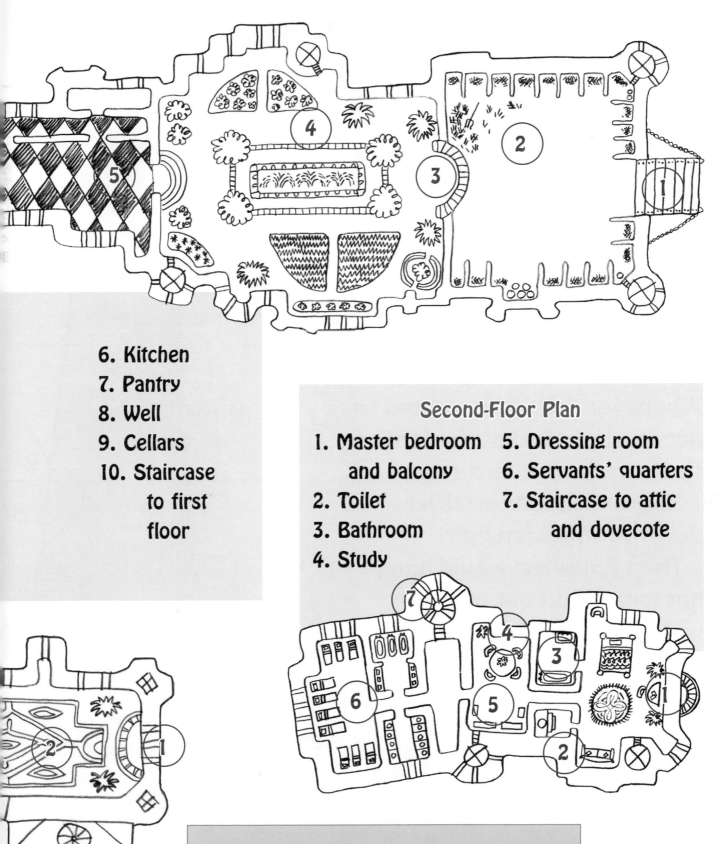

6. Kitchen
7. Pantry
8. Well
9. Cellars
10. Staircase
    to first
    floor

Second-Floor Plan

1. Master bedroom
   and balcony
2. Toilet
3. Bathroom
4. Study
5. Dressing room
6. Servants' quarters
7. Staircase to attic
   and dovecote

Now let's look at other fairytale homes...

Rapunzel's tower

Rapunzel was a sad and lonely princess. A wicked witch had shut her away in a tall tower in the middle of a forest.

The tower had no stairs or doors, only a tiny window at the very top. Whenever the witch wanted to get in, she stood at the foot of the tower and called out:

"Rapunzel, Rapunzel, let down your golden hair!"

Then Rapunzel would hang her long braid out of the window so the old witch could climb up her hair.

One day, as Rapunzel was singing out her window, a prince rode by and was enchanted by her song.

16

While he was trying to find a way in, he saw the witch climb up Rapunzel's braid.

"So that's the way up, is it?" said the prince to himself. "I think I'll come back later." That night, he went to the base of the tower and cried:

"Rapunzel, Rapunzel, let down your golden hair!"

When Rapunzel saw the prince she was very happy. Together, they planned an escape. Every time the prince came to see her, he brought her some silk thread, so she could weave a ladder.

But the witch discovered their plans and cut off Rapunzel's hair while the prince was climbing up. He fell into the thorn bushes below and then rode away, badly hurt.

By the time the prince had recovered and found his way back again, the old witch had died. And, luckily for Rapunzel, her hair had grown again, so the prince was able to help her make her escape at last.

Climbing towers

This old tower is made entirely from blocks of stone.

Once Rapunzel and her prince escaped, they needed a new home. Rapunzel had her heart set on a tower in the country (after all, that's what she was used to).

But before she picked one, she took time to look at all the towers for sale.

Modern skyscrapers, such as the Burj Khalifa in Dubai, are made from **steel** and **reinforced** concrete.

The Eiffel Tower in Paris, France, is made of criss-crossed bars of iron.

- Architect's words -

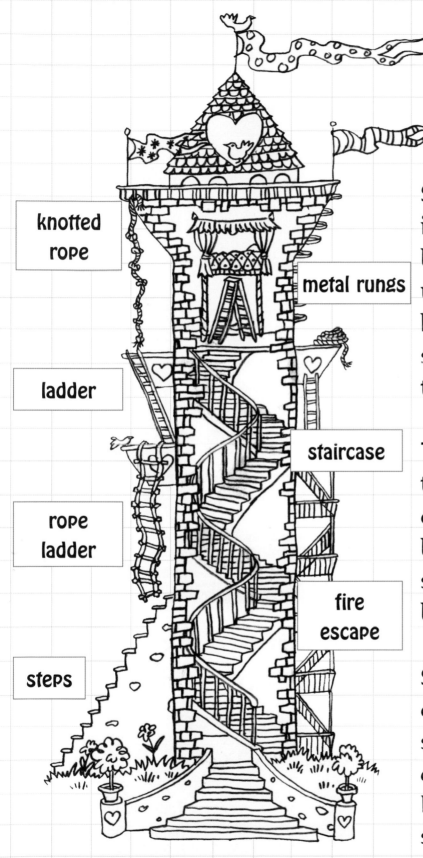

knotted rope

metal rungs

ladder

staircase

rope ladder

fire escape

steps

STAIRS: A set of steps inside or outside a building used for going up or down. Staircases have a frame for support and a railing to hold on to.

The stairs are often the strongest part of a building because they are supported by the building's structure.

Stone steps, fire escapes, and spiral staircases are all stairs. Ladders have steps called rungs.

19

The shoe house

A woman and her children want to live in this quirky shoe house! But how will they make it into a home? They need rooms where they can work, relax, and sleep.

This odd house is the Haines Shoe House in Hellam, York County, Pennsylvania, USA.

Architect's notebook
- Room layout -

The architect needs to divide the house up into several floors with stairs leading from one to the other.

What rooms would you expect to find in a family home? A living room where people can sit and talk and watch TV? A kitchen, a bathroom, and bedrooms for everyone? There may even be space for other rooms, such as a playroom, a laundry room, a storage room, and even an attic.

- Architect's words -

CROSS SECTION:
An architect makes a cross-section drawing to show the rooms and other spaces inside a house. The picture here looks as if a knife has cut right through the middle of the house.

A staircase must lead somewhere, a door must lead somewhere—every part of a house must connect.

Does this house work?

Answer these questions...

Maybe your layout wouldn't be quite as crazy as this shoe house—but this is a dream house, after all!

* When rain falls on the roof, it collects in a funnel and runs down a chute. Does the chute look like something you would see at a waterpark?

* There are two different ways of moving between floors. What are they?

* How many bedrooms are there?

* What's being made and sold in the **basement**?

* Why would the family pets like this house?

* Find the two places where you can wash up.

* Where could you relax and read a good book?

A lot has to fit into this home!

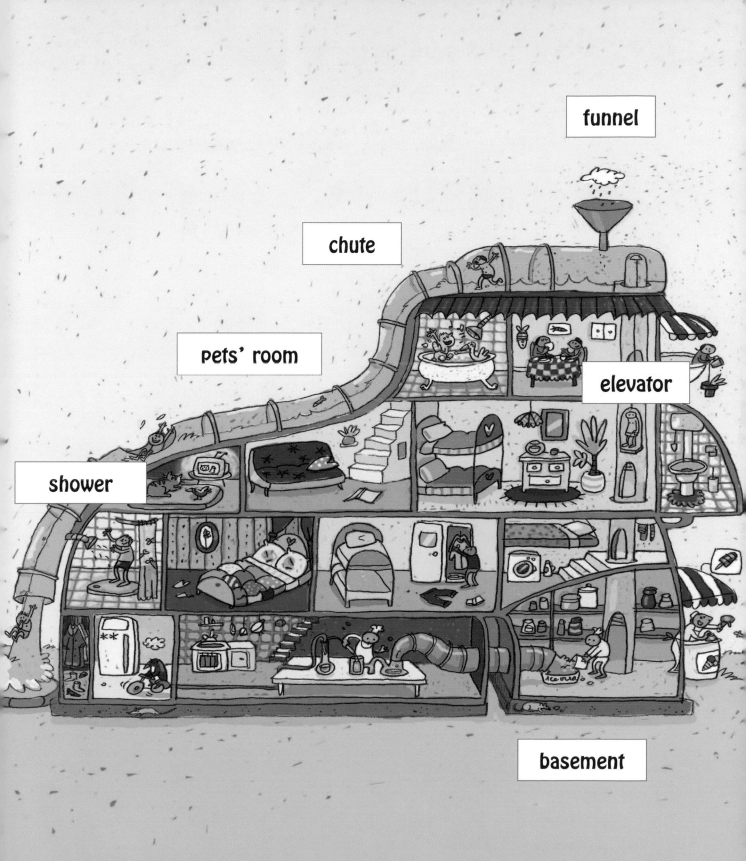

funnel

chute

pets' room

elevator

shower

basement

Hansel and Gretel cottage

Many people like to live in small cottages in the countryside, often in a village.

A cottage can be a very small home, either one or two **stories** high. Both ground and first floors may contain just two rooms, one on either side of a central staircase.

Many cottages are built using **natural materials**, with stone tiles on the floors, wooden **beams**, and straw **thatch** on the roof.

This cottage looks like the house in the fairy tale Hansel and Gretel. The "sweets" are colored stones and the "icing" is white paint.

A sweet story?

Hansel and Gretel were the children of a poor woodcutter who could not afford to feed his whole family. The woodcutter's wife decided to take the children deep into the forest and leave them there to look after themselves.

Hansel brought along breadcrumbs to make a trail to lead them home again. But birds ate the crumbs and the children were lost. Then, in the middle of the woods they found a strange house made of cakes and sweets. Hansel ate pieces of the sugary window while his sister munched on a creamy wall.

They ate and ate, until the door opened and out stepped an old woman.

She seemed kind at first, but she was actually a wicked witch. She planned to cook the children in her oven and eat them.

She locked Hansel in a cage and made Gretel work around the house. Then she lit the oven and waited for it to heat up. But when she opened the oven door to test the heat, Gretel quickly pushed her in and closed the door. Then Gretel ran to free her brother.

The children discovered a treasure in the witch's house and decided to fill their pockets with the jewels. Then they left and finally found their way home.

Their father was thrilled to see them. His cruel wife had died. And from that day on they lived happily ever after.

Three little pigs

The fairy tale of the Three Little Pigs is very famous. The story begins when the pigs are sent out into the world by their mother to "seek their fortune." Each pig decides to build a house.

Wood can be sawed into planks that are nailed together to form sturdy walls and a roof.

Reeds are a strong water plant. They can be cut and knotted together to form walls and a roof.

The first little pig builds a house of straw, but a wolf blows it down and eats the pig. The second pig builds a house of sticks, with the same result. But the third pig builds a house of tough **bricks**, and the wolf cannot blow it down. The wolf is so angry, he decides to slide down the chimney after the pig.

But the smart little pig boils a pot of water in the fireplace. The wolf lands in the pot when he slides down the chimney.

- Architect's words -

Which materials would you choose?

STRAW AND REEDS:
Straw and reeds are lightweight and easy to gather in the countryside.

WOOD:
Wood can be a good choice if you live near a forest.

BRICK:
Bricks are best if you want a strong, solid home.

Bricks are made of baked clay. They are stacked in rows and held together with cement. Clay tiles are overlapped on the roof.

29

Glossary

archway A curved structure, often used to support walls and roofs

basement The room in the bottom of a building, often below ground level

beam A strong piece of wood used to support parts of a building

brick A rectangular block made of a mixture of clay and other materials that has been hardened by heating

chandelier A lighting fixture that hangs from the ceiling usually with a number of branches containing lights or candles

concrete A mixture of cement, sand and other rocks that sets to a hard material

glass A tough material you can see through made from a mix of heated sand and other materials

limestone A kind of rock used in building, which can be easily shaped

marble A very hard rock that can be shaped

natural materials Various things that are not human-made, such as wood, grass, and stone

pillar A tall, slim, upright stone or metal support

plan An outline drawing, often made to scale, that shows how a building will be constructed

porous Able to soak up water

quarters Areas where people live

reinforced Having more strength

scale A way of measuring that allows big objects to be seen small

site A place or location where a building will be put

slate A tough stone that can be used as roof tiles

spire A tall, narrow structure that comes to a point, often built on the top of a tower

spit A rod that holds meat to cook over an open fire

steel A strong metal made of a mix of iron and other elements, used in building

steeple A tower that comes to a point and is built on the top of a roof

story Another name for a floor or level of a building

structure Another name for the framework of a building

tile A thin, flat slab of stone, brick or other material used to cover roofs, walls or floors

thatch Roofing material made of dried straw or grass

timber Another name for wood

Learning more

Books:

Building a Castle. Paul Humphrey.
  Arcturus Publishing, 2013.
Readers learn all about building a
medieval castle.

*Look At That Building! A First Book of
  Structures*. Scot Ritchie. Kids Can
  Press, 2011.
Five friends set out to build a doghouse
and explore basic construction concepts
including foundations, frames, and other
building fundamentals.

*The Three Little Pigs:
An Architectural Tale*.
  Steven Guarnaccia. Abrams, 2010.
This quirky picture book retells the
classic "tail" with each little pig
representing three famous architects:
Frank Gehry, Phillip Johnson, and Frank
Lloyd Wright.

Websites:

PBS's Building Big video and website:
  www.pbs.org/wgbh/buildingbig/
This website includes activities as it
explores bridges, skyscrapers, and more.

Archkidecture:
  www.archkidecture.org/
This website gives a lot of basic
information on architecture for kids.

The Great Buildings Collection:
  www.greatbuildings.com/
Readers receive design and architectural
information on a thousand buildings
from around the world.

Structures Around the World: Activities
for the Elementary Classroom:
  www.exploratorium.edu/structures/
Readers learn all about structures through
hands-on activities provided by the
Exploratorium museum.

Try Engineering:
www.tryengineering.org/lesson.php
This website features lessons plans and
activities that explore engineering principles.

Index